Lashing
vibes

JOURNAL FOR LASH TECHS

GD

MORNING
Be ♡ u ♡ Tiful

My lash prayer 🙏

What's your favorite vibe while lashing?

Will you practice today?

Date:

    Yes / No

Date:

    Yes / No

Date:

    Yes / No

What's your lashing goal?

My lashing goal for today is_____????

Date:

Goal:

Date
:
Goal
:

Date:

Goal:

Date:

Goal:

"Who needs
a boyfriend
when you have
the best set of
lashes."

Tiara
McDowell

My top 5 companies for products are?

1.

2.

3.

4.

5.

go to style is...

Natural

Open Eye

Cat Eye

Doll Eye

.......Continued

It takes me _____ hrs for classics!

It takes me _____ hrs for volume!

It takes me _____ hrs for a hybrid set!

Will you practice for 30 min today?

do you use lash map's?

Open eye

9 10 11 12 11 10 9

Kitten

8 9 10 11 12 11 10

Cat eye

9 10 11 12 13 14 13

Baby doll

10 11 12 12 12 12 11

Who is
your
favorite
client?

Who is your least favorite client?

mad about you

I love to use _____ products!

My weekly client goal is?

My best glue by far is ....

My weekly lash goal is?

Do you encourage self care of lashes?

Yes or No

I plan to lash (amount)_____ today

ADD INGREDIENTS IF DYI...

Do you buy lash cleaner, or prefer DYI?

love

My thoughts for today.........

I love to use _____ products!

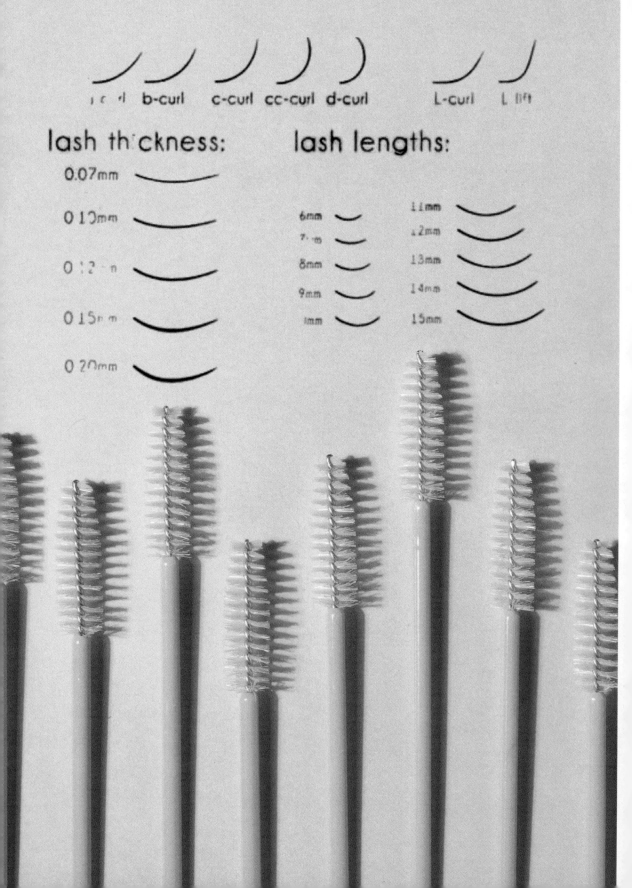

i-curl   b-curl   c-curl   cc-curl   d-curl   L-curl   L lift

lash thickness: lash lengths:

0.07mm

0.10mm   6mm   11mm
                              7mm   12mm
0.12mm   8mm   13mm
                              9mm   14mm
0.15mm   1mm   15mm

0.20mm

Which thickness do you prefer?

What is your favorite length to use?

All you need is
love.
But Lashes
every now and
then
doesn't hurt.

TIARA MCDOWELL

My weekly client goal is?

Lets keep those hands and fingers

working

(hand Exercises)

Take 10 mins

Shouts out to your fav Products!

My thoughts for today.........

My weekly client goal is?

love

Lash love is_____?

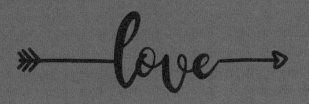

Breathe, smile, exhale you're beautiful!

TIARA MCDOWELL

Ex -ten- tac-toe

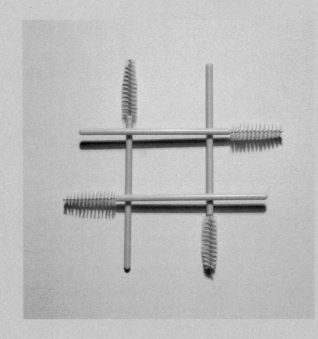

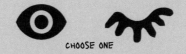

CHOOSE ONE

My thoughts for today.........

Lash practice today, for a perfect
lash tomorrow....

I store my glues like this !!!

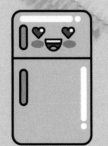

Lash Wash your hands!

ways I make my clients comfortable

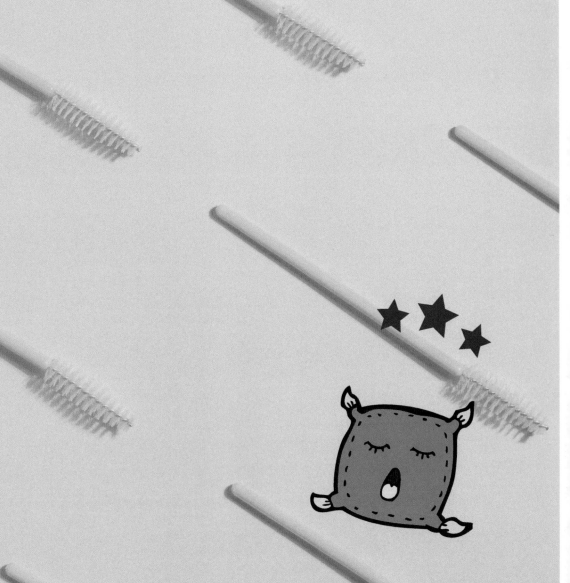

MY IDEAL WORK PLACE IS!!!

Promotions I plan use!!

What I'm trying to accomplish?...
besides this shmoney!

cat eye

natural

MESSY BUN

DOLLY

puppy dog

natural   spiked   kitten

messy bun

kitten

Circle your go to lash style

dolly

spiked

messy bun

puppy dog

kitten

puppy dog

cat eye

natural

Will you set aside 1hr today for practice?

Date:
start:
finish:

Date:
start:
finish:

Date:
start:
finish:

Shh...

Night thoughtz.........

If you want a thing bad enough to go
out and fight for it, to work day and
night for it, to give up your time, your
peace and sleep for it...If all that you
dream and scheme is about it,.. and life
seems useless and worthless without it..
If you gladly sweat for it and fret for it
and plan for it and lose all your terror of
the opposition for it ... If you simply go
after that thing that you want with all
your capacity, strength and sagacity,
faith hope and confidence and stern
pertinacity... If neither cold, poverty,
famine, nor gout , sickness nor pain, of
body and brain, can keep you beseech
and beset it, with the help of God,
YOU WILL GET IT !!!
-LES BROWN

live
your
dream.

You Can Accomplish
Anything

Made in the USA
Columbia, SC
30 April 2020